FUR TRAPPERS AND TRADERS
The Indians, the Pilgrims,
and the Beaver

Other Walker books by Beatrice Siegel:

INDIANS OF THE WOODLAND
A NEW LOOK AT THE PILGRIMS

SANTA ANA PUBLIC LIBRARY

J
973
SIE

FUR TRAPPERS AND TRADERS

The Indians, the Pilgrims, and the Beaver

by BEATRICE SIEGEL

Illustrated by William Sauts Bock

WALKER AND COMPANY/NEW YORK

TO MICHAEL AND SUMI

Library of Congress Cataloging in Publication Data

Siegel, Beatrice.
    Fur trappers and traders.

    Bibliography: p. 63 Index: p. 64
    SUMMARY: Describes the early fur trade in
the New World and discusses its influence on
North American history.
    1. Pilgrims (New Plymouth colony)—Juvenile
literature. 2. Fur trade—New England—
History—Juvenile literature. 3. Indians of
North America—New England—Hunting—
Juvenile literature. 4. Massachusetts—
History—New Plymouth, 1620–1691—Juvenile
literature. [1. Fur trade—New England—
History. 2. Pilgrims (New Plymouth colony)
3. Indians of North America—New England]
I. Bock, William Sauts, 1939–   II. Title.
F68.S564   1981   974.4′02   80-7671
ISBN 0–8027–6396–0
ISBN 0–8027–6397–9 (lib. bdg.)

Text copyright © 1981 by BEATRICE SIEGEL
Illustrations copyright © 1981 by William Sauts Bock

All rights reserved. No part of this book may be reproduced or transmitted in any form or by an means, electric or mechanical, including photocopying, recording or by any information storage and retrieval system, without permission in writing form the Publisher.

First published in the United States of America in 1981 by the Walker Publishing Company, Inc.

Reprinted 1987.

Published simultaneously in Canada by Beaverbooks, Limited, Don Mills, Ontario.

Trade ISBN: 0-8027-6396-0
Reinf. ISBN: 0-8027-6397-9

Library of Congress Catalog Card Number: 80-7671

Printed in the United States of America

10 9 8 7 6 5 4 3 2

Book design by LENA FONG HOR

CONTENTS

INTRODUCTION: THE COCKED HAT

THE DUKE OF BUCKINGHAM strode into court to visit his king, James I of England. He cut a handsome figure. In that period of the 1620s, his extravagant clothes were made of velvet and brocade and trimmed with satin and lace. Nothing, however, was as splendid as his hat.

It was a cocked hat—high in the crown, broad-brimmed, and turned up and fastened to one side with a golden jeweled clasp. A long ostrich feather swooped out of the silken band and curled gracefully downward. The hat was soft and furry. No wonder! For it was a felt cloth hat, made from the pelts of beaver.

Both men and women of fashion wore these beaver felt hats. They were symbols of status and wealth and were worn outdoors as well as indoors, at church and at the table. Only in the presence of royalty were these hats removed—or doffed. Over the years they came in different styles: broad-brimmed or narrow; tall-crowned, flat, or peaked; gem-studded, embroidered, or plain.

"Beavers," as these hats were called, were so valuable that the rich left them as bequests in wills. And highway thieves waylaid aristocrats and gentry to rob them of their hats.

As early as the fourteenth century, the merchants of Europe needed beaver pelts to meet the craze in felt hats. Imagine the excitement when explorers reported that the forests of the New World sheltered millions and millions of beaver and other fur-bearing animals.

This book tells how the Pilgrims joined the fur rush in the New World and sent beaver pelts back to England. In questions and answers we will show how the pursuit of the beaver gave shape and direction to early North American history.

1625

1605

1630

1610

1638

BEAVER HATS

1610

1600

BEAVERS AT WORK

WHAT KIND OF ANIMAL IS THE BEAVER?

THE BEAVER BELONGS to a large family of animals called rodents. It shares many qualities in common with its cousins the muskrat, the squirrel, the chipmunk, the rat, and hundreds of other relatives. In particular, the beaver has the family's large, chisel-sharp four front teeth. It uses those teeth, its strong neck muscles, and flat broad tail in its skills as a builder.

The beaver constructs its home, or lodge, in streams, lakes, and brooks. It gnaws down stout trees and drags branches, stone, leaves, grasses, and whatever else is lying around, to its underwater homesite. Mud is used to cement these materials together. Then, working through the night ("busy as a beaver"), it dams up the water and builds a strong, secure home for itself and immediate family (its mate and young).

The beaver is safe in its lodge underneath the water from all its enemies except man.

WHY WERE ANIMALS HUNTED?

Fur-bearing animals were valued throughout the ages. Their meat provided food, and their skins were used as clothes and robes for warmth.

As nations developed in the Old World, kings, queens, and wealthy families demanded the comfort of rich furs. Rare ermine and sable were fashioned into luxurious robes or used as trim on garments. The poor warmed themselves in common rabbit skins.

The Indians of the New World trapped animals for their immediate needs. Their religion tied them to the earth by teaching them to cherish everything in nature. They felt at one with their surroundings and could find their way through dense forests in all seasons and weather. The habits of animals were as familiar to them as members of their own families.

WHAT WAS SPECIAL ABOUT THE BEAVER?

The beaver was always prized for special qualities. Two large glands near the rectum gave off a sweet-scented musky oil. This oil was used in earlier times to treat ailments. It was supposed to cure toothache, earache, epilepsy, frostbite, colds, and hysteria. It was also used to hold the odor in perfumes.

But the extraordinary value of the beaver was in its pelt. Underneath the outer layer of long, coarse hairs, the beaver has a thick, soft, downy underfur covered with tiny barbs. When the fur is removed from the hide and treated with a special process of heat and pressure, the barbs stick together—interlock—and the fur is converted into a felt cloth. The cloth is light in weight, pliable, lustrous, and very strong. It can last for years.

The felt cloth triggered new styles in hats. By the 1400s, beaver felt hats became the style among the wealthy. Hatters and fur merchants did a brisk business catering to the new fashions.

WHAT HAPPENED TO THE BEAVER IN EUROPE?

Throughout the vast forests of Europe, from Russia to France and Spain, the beaver and other fur-bearing animals were hunted mercilessly. (No one thought at that time about conservation.)

Not only were the animals killed off, but the forests that gave them food and shelter were cut down. When cities became crowded, people spread out into the countryside. They cleared the land and used the timber to build homes and heat them. Industries such as ship building required lumber.

The beaver, once plentiful, became a rare animal by the end of the 1500s. The European hat trade, dependent on beaver pelts, came to a standstill.

WHAT NEWS SPREAD THROUGH EUROPE?

By 1600 WORD HAD SPREAD to the courts and counting houses of Europe that rich, precious furs—as valuable as gold—were to be found in the dense woodlands of the New World. Profits could be made, the reports said, and the Indians were eager for trade.

The first to bring such news were French and Spanish fishermen. Long before Columbus's discovery, they had sailed their small wooden vessels to Newfoundland. There along the northeast coast of the New World they found codfish. For months they lived in huts along the shore while they dried and salted down their catch. They built warehouses to store their supply until the voyage home. Local Indians came to their huts and entered into simple barter, or the exchange of merchandise. The Indian took the fur robe

FUR PELTS READY TO BE SHIPPED

off his back and gave it to the fisherman. In exchange for it, the fisherman gave the Indian a metal knife or a copper pot or an iron hatchet.

When the fishermen returned to their hometowns, they sold the fur pieces in the market place and made a good profit. Many gave up fishing for the more profitable fur trade.

French explorers also did business with the Indians. They gathered together thousands of fur skins as they penetrated into parts of Canada and Maine that they called New France.

It was later estimated that more than fifty million beaver and other fur-bearing animals lived in the forests between the Atlantic and the Pacific Oceans and from the Arctic to the Gulf of California.

WHEN DID THE ENGLISH ENTER THE FUR TRADE?

The English were latecomers to the fur trade. When they realized the wealth to be made, English explorers not only charted the harbors of the New World but looked into the possibilities of trade.

Bartholomew Gosnold, in 1602, searched New England for sassafras, a food flavoring, and also traded with the Indians for fur. A year after that, explorer Martin Pring, and later, George Weymouth, returned to England from New World voyages laden down with barrels full of "Beaver skins, Otter skins, Sable and other small skins."

Captain John Smith sailed along the north Atlantic coast in 1614 and exchanged "for trifles . . . 1100 Beaver skins and other skins." He already knew that fur traders in the Virginia colony were carrying on a profitable business at Chesapeake Bay.

WHAT DID CAPTAIN SMITH RECOMMEND?

Smith, as well as other explorers, recommended that the English send colonists to the coast of the New World. They encouraged settlements in order to reap the riches of the forests and the waters—fur, fish, and timber.

English merchants and noblemen, looking for profitable businesses, had already begun to corner New World land. The more powerful among them, through connections at the courts of Queen Elizabeth I and King James I, had won charters to huge tracts. They looked for bold, adventurous settlers to occupy the land, claim it, and enter into trade with the Indians.

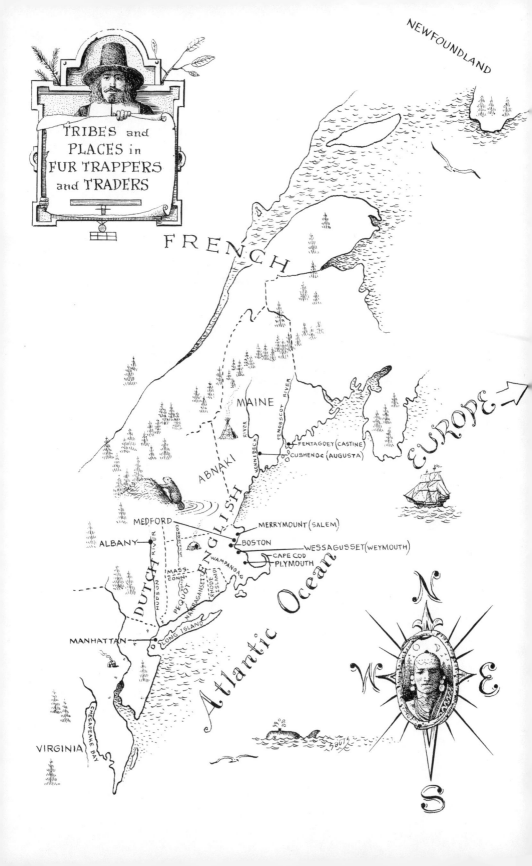

NEWFOUNDLAND

TRIBES and PLACES in FUR TRAPPERS and TRADERS

FRENCH

ENGLISH

EUROPE →

MAINE

KENNEBEC RIVER

PENOBSCOT RIVER

PENTAGOET (CASTINE)

CUSHENOC (AUGUSTA)

ABNAKI

MEDFORD

MERRYMOUNT (SALEM)

ALBANY

BOSTON

WESSAGUSSET (WEYMOUTH)

CONNECTICUT

CAPE COD
PLYMOUTH

WAMPANOAG

HUDSON RIVER

DUTCH

MASS.
CONN.

PEQUOT

RHODE ISLAND

NARRAGANSETT

LONG ISLAND

Atlantic Ocean

MANHATTAN

CHESAPEAKE BAY

VIRGINIA

N
W E
S

HOW DID
THE PILGRIMS
FIT INTO
ENGLAND'S PLANS?

THE NEED FOR SETTLERS in the New World opened the way for a group of people we know as the Pilgrims. For religious and other motives, the Pilgrims had decided to build a settlement in the New World. In order to do so, however, they had to become part of a business deal.

They had no money for the voyage they planned in 1620. Along came Thomas Weston, an English merchant. He organized seventy English businessmen into a trading company to back the Pilgrim voyage and colony. They put up the money to charter a ship, the *Mayflower*, and they stocked it with food and other supplies. Among the supplies were cloth, beads, knives, and other items for the Indian trade.

The Pilgrims agreed to a contract with the merchants. In exchange for their financial backing, they promised to work hard and send ships laden with merchandise back to England.

The merchants knew of the ready market for beaver skins and urged the colonists to enter into trade with the Indians at once. They convinced the colonists that they would keep them supplied with food, clothing, and trading items.

WHAT WAS "THAT WONDERFUL PLAGUE?"

Before the Pilgrims landed in Plymouth in 1620, other European explorers and fishermen had stopped off along the New England coast and infected Indians with their diseases.

After one such visit by Europeans in 1616–1617, a terrible pestilence broke out in New England. It may have been typhus or typhoid fever. Unlike Europeans, who knew of plague and pestilence, the Indians had no such previous experience. They did not know that disease could quickly spread from a sick person to a healthy one. Their herbal remedies were useless. And they had not yet built up natural resistance to a foreign disease. Sickness swept over them like a supernatural force before which they and their leaders were helpless.

The disease wiped out whole villages of Indians from Cape Cod in Massachusetts to the Penobscot

River in Maine. Those who survived could barely hold together the structure of their lives. The death of hunters left them short of food. The death of warriors made them prey to stronger tribes.

King James I of England called it "That Wonderful Plague among the Savages" because the Indians were so ravaged that even in 1620, three years after the onset of the disease, they did not have the strength to resist the colonization of their land.

The Pilgrims, however, were in no better condition. They were going through the "starving period." During the first months after their landing at Plymouth, many died from hunger and illness. Of the 102 who

made the voyage, only 52 remained—a frightened, hungry band, hugging the coast of Plymouth.

Weakened settlers faced weakened Indians. Nevertheless, the Indians helped the Pilgrims and taught them how to plant new crops. And though they were afraid of each other, they started to trade.

The Wampanoags, coastal tribes, had bartered fur pieces with European fishermen and explorers, and they wanted European products.

WHY DID THE PILGRIMS HAVE TO DEPEND ON THE FUR TRADE?

The Pilgrims desperately needed food and clothing for themselves as well as goods for the Indian trade. But only when they shipped fur and other merchandise back to England would they receive cargoes of supplies in return.

As soon as they built shelters against the winter, the Pilgrims entered into trade with the Indians. Many of them had never seen beaver pelts and knew nothing about the fur trade. But they said to the Indian Samoset, when he visited at Plymouth, "Bring in the neighboring Indians with such beaver skins as they had to truck (trade)."

Samoset and Squanto were two Indians who became loyal friends of the Pilgrims. They acted as guides and interpreters when they led the Pilgrims inland to ex-

AN INDIAN VISITING THE PILGRIMS

pand their trade. When a Pilgrim child became lost in the dense forests, these two spread word to the nearby tribes. The child was always found and returned to the colony. They also paved the way for the Pilgrims to meet members of the Wampanoag tribes and especially their chief, Massasoit, who had jurisdiction over the land on which they had settled.

DID THE ENGLISH MERCHANTS
HELP THE PILGRIMS?

The English merchants kept the Pilgrims in such short supply that they had to scrounge for food during the first few years. And in order to get knives, beads, and cloth for the fur trade, they often sold off precious beaver skins to trading ships that happened to stop in port.

*INDIAN WOMEN EXCHANGING FUR ROBES FOR
"TRINKETS"*

WHAT HAPPENED TO
THE PILGRIMS' FIRST CARGO?

By the time the Pilgrims settled in Plymouth, much
of the beaver had already been wiped out along the
coast. They had to explore other regions for trade.

In September 1621, less than a year after they
landed, the Pilgrims sent a group of armed men, with
Squanto as interpreter, north in a small ship to Boston

harbor. A bit inland, in the present town of Medford, they came upon Indian women who gave them fur robes in exchange for "trinkets." The group gathered together a good supply of beaver and returned to Plymouth.

Two months later, in November, they loaded onto a ship known as the *Fortune* two hogsheads, or barrels, of beaver and other skins as well as a cargo of lumber for the return voyage to England. They figured that the fur skins, the most valuable part of the cargo, would help pay off half the debt to the English merchants and earn for them a return supply of needed goods.

The *Fortune* never arrived in England! A French pirate ship attacked the English ship at sea and stole its cargo.

The Pilgrims still owed the merchants the full amount of the debt.

A year later, in 1622, the colonists sent "all the beaver and other furs they had" on the ship the *Anne*. Thereafter, there were frequent shipments of beaver and other furs to England. As Governor Bradford said, "There was no other means to purchase the food which they so much wanted and clothes also."

Within the first few years it became clear to the Pilgrims that their existence depended on the fur trade.

WERE THERE OTHER ENGLISH FUR TRADERS?

ACCORDING TO THE OFFICIAL GRANT, the Pilgrims had a monopoly over the New England land between Plymouth and Boston. The Pilgrims figured it gave them exclusive rights to the fur trade in that region. Nevertheless, interloping traders set up posts along the coast. Often they disregarded the royal decree that prohibited trade without a license.

One of the first rivals for the fur trade was Thomas Weston, the same man who had helped the Pilgrims get financial backing for their colony. In 1622, Weston sold his share of the business in England and received a patent to set up a trading post in Wessagusset (now Weymouth), south of Boston Bay.

Weston brought in a group of adventurers different from the Pilgrims in every way. They had no firm religious beliefs, did not believe in hard work, and in general looked for an easy way to earn money. To keep from starving, they stole corn from the Indians or depended on the Pilgrims' scanty food supply.

At first the Pilgrims tried to be helpful. But they found these adventurers to be "rude fellows" and "not fit for an honest man's company."

The worst thing these settlers did, however, was to cut into the Pilgrim fur trade with the local Indians. They also interfered with the fur supplies that came down from the north.

WHY WERE THE INDIANS MASSACRED AT WESSAGUSSET?

The Pilgrims worked out a way to put an end to Weston's trading post and the competition. They spread word that the Indians at Wessagusset were conspiring to wipe out the settlers. (This claim was never proven.) To "save" the colony, Myles Standish, head of the Plymouth militia, led a group of eight heavily armed men to Wessagusset. He pretended he came there to trade with the Indians.

The Indians did not trust Standish. They knew he had a vile temper and that he was savage with his sword. Nevertheless, Wittuwamat, an outstanding warrior, taunted Standish and his men. He flashed his knife and boasted he had killed French and English.

THE HEAD OF WITTUWAMAT

He heaped further insults on the English. He called them weak, "especially," he said, because "they died crying, making sour faces, more like children than men."

Despite their feeling that Standish meant to harm them, the Indians visited Standish in his hut, where they were promised a feast. Among them were Peksuot, known as a "man of valor," Wittuwamat, his fifteen-year-old brother, and another warrior. As these men entered the hut, Standish and his militia fell on the Indians and killed three of them in bloody fighting. They grabbed the young boy, took him outdoors, and hanged him in full view of his friends.

The terrorized Indians fled to the swamps to hide. Standish commanded his men to pursue them and put all warriors to death.

Standish then ordered his men to cut off the head of Wittuwamat and mount it on a spike. Bearing the head like a banner, Standish and his group returned to Plymouth. The Pilgrims put the cut-off head on display on top of Plymouth Fort. It warned all Indians of their fate if the Pilgrims found them troublesome.

Hatred of Standish and the English swept through the Indian tribes. In a rage, the Indians killed some Wessagusset settlers. The survivors closed down the colony and fled north to Maine. They turned down Standish's invitation to join them at Plymouth.

THE MAYPOLE AT MERRYMOUNT

WHAT HAPPENED AT MERRYMOUNT?

Despite the massacre at Wessagusset, the Pilgrims were not free of competition for long. A few years later another colony threatened their survival.

Thomas Morton, a lawyer educated in England, set up a trading post near Wessagusset and called it Merrymount (now Salem). Morton, a merry soul, liked to have a good time. His trading post became known as a gay, roguish place where traders could drink, sing, gamble, and dance at the Maypole Morton had erected. He also welcomed Indian trappers, to whom he sold guns and powder.

The Pilgrims felt threatened by the goings-on at Merrymount. Their young people found it difficult to lead a strict life. Many preferred the "sinful" activity at Merrymount.

The Pilgrims thought that the traffic in guns to the Indians would endanger their security.

And Morton, popular with traders and trappers, was filling his warehouses with thousands of beaver skins.

The Pilgrims complained that the economic existence of their colony was at stake. They charged Morton with breaking the law that prohibited the sale of guns to the Indians.

Again Captain Standish came to the fore. He led a brigade of armed men to Merrymount to arrest Morton. After a fight, Standish captured Morton and brought him back to Plymouth to stand trial. The Pilgrim leaders tried to have Morton hanged, but influential friends put a stop to that. As punishment, Morton was shipped back to England.

By their "outrageous act," Morton wrote later, the Pilgrims made themselves masters of Merrymount and added "to their glory."

WHO ELSE COMPETED FOR THE FUR TRADE?

THE FRENCH AND DUTCH WERE well-established fur traders by the time the Pilgrims put down roots. They had staked out land that was handed to them by their kings just as the English did.

Often everyone claimed a monopoly over the same territory. These conflicting claims turned New England into a hotbed of political and economic rivalries. Traders schemed to outwit each other and intercept each other's trade. They spread out into the wilderness and carved new frontiers in order to gain control over fresh supplies.

The Indians, the real residents of the land, became the victims. In the end, the beaver trade, violence, and wars would contribute to their destruction.

THE DUTCH ON MANHATTAN ISLAND

WHERE WERE THE DUTCH?

The Dutch started their adventure in the New World in 1609 when Henry Hudson sailed his ship the *Half Moon* up the river that bears his name (the Hudson River) as far north as Albany. By the early 1620s, the Dutch took over the island of Manhattan. From there, they spread their domination east to Long Island.

They were also well entrenched in Rhode Island. The Pilgrims discovered this when they sent an excursion south to do business with the Narragansett Indians. Governor William Bradford announced that the land south of Plymouth belonged to them, but no one listened. The Dutch and the Narragansetts continued their profitable trade.

When the Pilgrims looked for trade in the Connecticut River Valley, they found that the Dutch had preceded them there, too, and had developed good trading relations with the Pequot Indians.

By 1624, the Dutch were shipping thousands of beaver skins to Europe.

HOW DID THE DUTCH
HANDLE THE PILGRIM FUR TRADE?

To encourage the Pilgrims to search for trade in other regions, the Dutch sold them wampum. Wampum were tiny flat beads skillfully carved out of the insides of certain shells. These shells, the periwinkle and the quahog, were not found north of Cape Cod. But they were valued by all northeastern tribes, especially those in Maine, who did not have a natural source of supply.

Indians used wampum for many purposes: in religious and official ceremonies, sewn together into peace belts, or made into personal ornaments. Wampum was also used as money—or as a means of exchange.

By 1625, the Pilgrims had already begun to trade on the Kennebec River in Maine. But when they added wampum to their trading supplies, it gave them access to other Maine tribes.

WHAT ABOUT THE FRENCH?

The French challenged the Pilgrims' rights to trade so far north. Their explorers and traders had started as early as 1535, and they claimed the northern part of the New World down into Maine for New France. Despite French protests, the Pilgrims carried on a thriving business with the Maine Indians, who had become their chief suppliers.

WAMPUM

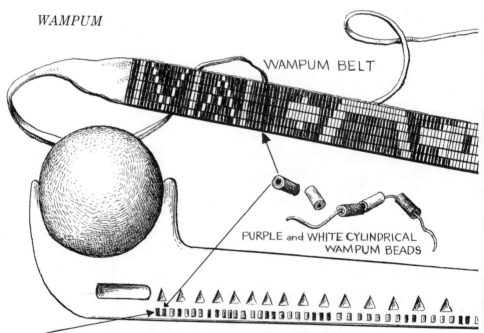

WAMPUM BELT

PURPLE and WHITE CYLINDRICAL WAMPUM BEADS

WAMPUM BEAD DECORATIONS ON A WAR CLUB

WERE THERE OTHER ENGLISH COMPETITORS?

In 1630, a band of nearly a thousand English colonists, whom we know as the Puritans, took over the region around Boston and established Boston Bay Colony. Many of these English settlers were wealthy (unlike the poor struggling Pilgrims) and had influence with the merchants and political leaders of England. Their strong, well-financed colony already included imaginative, aggressive business leaders who became powerful rivals for the New England fur trade.

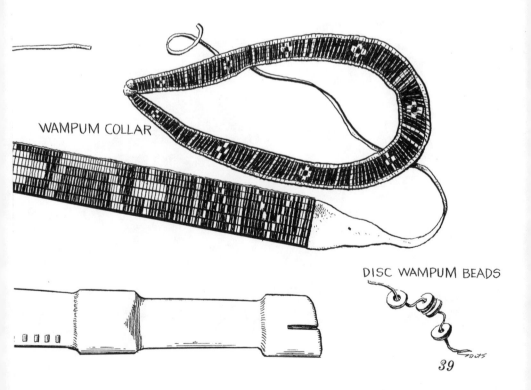

WAMPUM COLLAR

DISC WAMPUM BEADS

PILGRIMS MEETING OTHER TRADERS

WHO WERE
"THE UNDERTAKERS?"

In 1627, A GROUP OF PILGRIM leaders formed their own trading company. Among them were William Bradford, William Brewster, Myles Standish, Isaac Allerton, Edward Winslow, and John Alden. They obtained

exclusive rights to the fur trade and all other business dealings of Plymouth Colony for a period of six years. For these privileges, they undertook (and are therefore called "The Undertakers") to pay off the colony's debts to the English merchants.

These Pilgrim leaders developed into clever, bold businessmen. They were the ones who expanded the Plymouth fur trade into the northern wilderness of Maine, where they did a thriving business with the Abnaki Indians. They set up warehouses in Cushenoc (now Augusta) and on the Penobscot River at Pentagoet (now Castine).

They pushed west and built trucking stations in the Connecticut River Valley, where they challenged the Dutch.

Plymouth traders would return from these excursions into Maine and Connecticut laden down with thousands of pounds of beaver skins and other furs.

The Undertakers reaped amazing profits. They paid off the debt to the English merchants, brought over other members of their congregation, and bought supplies for the colony.

During the period of their monopoly, the Undertakers themselves accumulated property and became rich, according to the standards of their day.

WHO DID
THE TRAPPING?

ENGLISH, FRENCH, AND DUTCH settlers did not hunt the beaver. This was carried out by the Indians. They were the trappers. Without the Indians there would not have been a fur trade. Before the European invasion, they trapped animals only for their immediate needs—for food, and for robes and clothing. The Indians who became part of the fur trade trapped animals for commercial purposes, to supply the fur and hat markets of Europe.

In the early days, trappers hunted the beaver without concern for conservation. Later on, in the 1700s, some tribes regulated the seasons and limits of hunting so that the beaver could continue to breed.

The Indian trappers were the real pioneers, the trail blazers. They opened up this country to exploration and discovery. They cut new trails and beat their way over mountains, across valleys and rivers. Deep in the interior they engaged other tribes as trappers. They

INDIAN TRAPPERS

45

1. SCRAPING THE HIDE CLEAN

PREPARING THE FUR PELTS

2. RUBBING THE HIDE WITH MARROW

would meet each other along lonely waterways where trappers of the interior would turn over their haul of beaver skins to the coastal Indians.

WHO PREPARED THE FUR?

Indians lived for months at hunting sites. Trapping the beaver was only one step in the preparation of fur for the trade. They also skinned the animals and separated the valuable parts of fur from the whole skin.

The hunters then hauled these pelts back to their villages. There women and children worked with them

3. THE SCRAPED AND MARROW-RUBBED HIDE DRIED ON ITS STRETCHING FRAME

and dressed the skins further, putting them through a curing and tanning process.

All this work was skilled, difficult, and time-consuming.

By the time the Indian trapper brought fur pelts to the trading posts, the pelts were ready to be loaded onto ships and sent to European markets.

WHO FOLLOWED THE TRAPPER?

The European demand for fur was inexhaustible. Beaver pelts were the basic raw material for the booming felt hat industry. England had become the center of the trade and was shipping beavers to all parts of Europe.

The fur trader, who shipped the pelts abroad, followed closely on the heels of the trappers. They kept Indian trappers on the move and forced them to open new frontiers. The traders drove a hard bargain. They were tough men, experienced in the competitive business world of Europe. Indians gave them furs that were usually far more valuable than the merchandise they received.

WHY DID THE INDIANS BECOME TRAPPERS?

Imagine the excitement of the Indian who held a steel knife in his hands for the first time! Or cloth—with which families could make clothes without curing and tanning the hides of animals. Or sharp, strong iron tools to work their fields. Or guns with which to hunt instead of bows and arrows.

These were products of an Iron Age Indians knew nothing about before Europeans invaded their land.

Indians had lived in a Stone Age culture. They carved their tools, bowls, and pots out of stone, wood, bone, or shell. It took days of difficult, tedious labor to make these products. They were perishable, broke easily, and had constantly to be replaced.

Iron Age products, called "trifles" or "trinkets" by

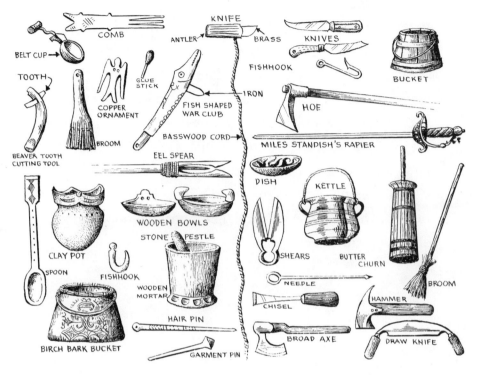

INDIAN PRODUCTS   *EUROPEAN PRODUCTS*

Europeans, were miracles to the Indians. They thought the English were foolish. "The English have no sense," they said. "They give us twenty knives like this for one beaver skin."

As demands for fur increased, however, the Indians also demanded a wider range of merchandise. In 1603, explorer Martin Pring reported that in exchange for barrels of fur, the Indians wanted "hooks, knives, scissors, hammers, nails, chisels, fishhooks, bells, beads, bugles, looking glasses, thimbles, pins, needles, thread and such like." They also asked for blankets and cloth.

Many tribes became dependent on ironware. They could no more turn back to stone and bone tools than people today could travel by horse and carriage instead of plane, train, or automobile. Or read by the oil lamp instead of electric light.

In time, many Indians forgot how to make their tools in the Stone Age way. They became dependent on European merchandise.

WHO BECAME RICH FROM THE FUR TRADE?

SOME INDIAN TRIBES became wealthier than others. Indians individually, however, did not become rich. They did not believe in accumulating personal wealth. Possessions were shared by all members of the tribe.

The fur trade made the Pilgrims, Puritans, and other settlers rich and brought fabulous wealth to England. French and Dutch traders and their countries also reaped fortunes.

The Pilgrims could never understand the customs of the Indians and especially their refusal to acquire wealth. They said the Indians had no foresight and would not save toward a time of need.

Indians, on the other hand, could not understand the drive of the English to pile up more possessions than they personally could use. Particularly strange to the Indians was the refusal of the English to share their wealth with those in need.

"What use are all these knives to you?" an Indian asked a fur trader. "Is not one enough with which to cut your meat? It is only your wicked heart that prevents you from giving them to us. Do you not see that the village has none?"

WHAT HAPPENED
TO THE INDIANS?

THE INDIAN WORLD began to shatter. It could not withstand the blows dealt it by the invading Europeans and their alien culture.

European competition for the fur trade sowed seeds of violence among Indian tribes. They became pawns in the hands of Europeans. Tribal wars became brutal and reflected European rivalries.

Trapping animals for the commercial market further weakened the ties of the Indians to their traditional ways of life.

Their independent economy gave way to dependence on European products.

Missionaries tried to make them Christians and divided them even more.

They suffered from alcoholism and the ravages of European diseases.

DID THE PILGRIMS HELP THE INDIANS?

Though the Pilgrims had survived only with the help of the Indians, they continued to regard the Indians as inferior and savage people.

The fur trade, which became the first successful business venture of Plymouth Colony, depended wholly on the cooperation of the Indians.

Nevertheless, neither the Pilgrims nor other European colonists ever helped the Indians find their way in the changing world. New laws and institutions regularly discriminated against them in education, in jobs, and in the courts. They were forced out of their own land.

By the time Indian tribes united to fight against the invaders, it was too late. The Indians suffered terrible defeats in the Pequot War (1637) and in King Philip's War (1675). Many were sold off as slaves. Others became as "scattered as autumnal leaves before the wind."

CHRISTIAN MISSIONARY AMONG THE INDIANS

Toward the end of the 1600's the fur trade had moved west, where the drive would continue to control fur-rich land.

By then new generations of New England settlers (Euro-Americans) had turned to other things. They became farmers or created new industries.

THE SPREAD OF SETTLEMENTS

1654

BEAVER ON SEAL OF
DUTCH
FUR TRADING POST

BEAVER ON DUTCH
NEW
NETHERLAND
SEAL

1623

BEAVER ON HUDSON'S

*AND THE
BEAVER?*

1686

BEAVER ON BRITISH
SEAL OF
NEW YORK CITY

BAY ARMS

BEAVER
ON MODERN
NEW YORK CITY SEAL

1915

BEAVER FELT IS NO LONGER the cloth from which elegant hats are made. Those manufactured today are very expensive and adorn the heads of Texas ranchers. They are also worn by the leaders of a religious sect called Hasidim.

Today beavers are hunted for fur coats, but conservation laws protect them so that they can never be wiped out. They have staged such a successful comeback that no state lists them as an endangered species. Families of beaver can again be found gnawing down trees, damming up brooks, and building underwater lodges.

The beaver has been honored in many ways for its crucial role in history. The French had struck a coin for Castorland or the "Land of the Beaver." To honor their trading posts in the early days, both the British and Dutch adopted seals with the image of the beaver. Even as late as 1915, the official seal of New York City included a beaver. Everywhere one will come across name places such as Beaver Pond, Beaver Meadow, Beaver Lodge, and Beaver River.

These are reminders of the rodent who became a force in history. From the earliest days, the fur trade helped shape events in North America. It opened up the west, caused violence and wars, contributed to the destruction of the Indian people, and brought fabulous wealth to European settlers and to western Europe.

The beaver is still a symbol of the North American fur trade.

NOTES

12 The beaver glandular secretion is called *castoreum*. It has been found that castoreum contains salicylic acid, a main ingredient in aspirin. No wonder castoreum was helpful in treating illness.

Castoreum is still used as a fixative in perfume.

21 You can find a fuller explanation of the business arrangement between the Pilgrims and the merchants in *A New Look at the Pilgrims: Why They Came to America,* by Beatrice Siegel.

22 King James I called it "That Wonderful Plague" in 1620 when he granted the Great Patent to the Council of New England. He added, the time was ready that "these large and goodly territories . . . [meaning the New World] shall be possessed and enjoyed" by the English.

30 Dr. Thomas Boylston Adams, for many years president of the Massachusetts Historical Society, is one of the scholars who questions the "plot" of the Indians. He claims the plot was never confirmed and said so at a talk to the Thomas Jefferson Memorial Foundation in 1958. That talk has been reprinted in a booklet called *The Crime of the Pilgrims.*

Dr. Adams also points out that the beloved minister of the Pilgrims, the Reverend John Robinson, protested the "killing of the poor Indians" and expressed his concern about Standish and the Plymouth militia. "There is cause to fear," he said, that "these may be wanting that tenderness of the life of man . . . which is meet."

37   For further reading about wampum, see Beatrice Siegel, *Indians of the Woodland,* pages 20 and 21.

43   American beaver trappers were called "Mountain Men." They learned their skills from the Indians and became a fierce, independent breed of men, who helped open up the West.

The early French settlers who did trapping without a license were called *coureurs de bois* or "runners in the woods."

54   Tecumseh, a Shawnee chief and a great leader, spoke before a council of midwest Indian tribes in 1812 and urged them to unite against the westward sweep of the colonialists. He said, "They [the whites] will soon conquer us apart and disunited, and we will be driven away from our native country and scattered as autumnal leaves before the wind."

59   Beaver felt hats still show up. A story in the *New York Times,* August 18, 1979, tells about a ninety-five-year-old man who came to court in a "handsome 60-year-old gray felt hat made of beaver fur."

60   *Castor* is the French word for beaver. Castorland, complete with zip code (13620) still exists in upper New York State, where the French once had a colony.

SUGGESTED READINGS

Burger, Carl. *Beaver Skins and Mountain Men.* New York: E. P. Dutton and Co., 1968.

Honig, Donald. *Frontiers of Fortune, the Fur Trade.* New York: McGraw-Hill Book Co., 1967.

Jones, Evan, and Morgan, Dale M. *Trappers and Mountain Men.* American Heritage. New York: Harper and Row, 1961.

Poling, James. *Beavers (A First Book), Their Extraordinary Lives and Curious History.* New York: Franklin Watts and Co., 1975.

Rich, Louise Dickson. *King Philip's War, 1675–76.* New York: Franklin Watts and Co., 1972.

Rounds, Glen. *The Beaver, How He Works.* New York: Holiday House, 1976.

Siegel, Beatrice. *Indians of the Woodland, Before and After the Pilgrims.* New York, Walker and Co., 1972.

Siegel, Beatrice. *A New Look at the Pilgrims, Why They Came to America.* New York: Walker and Co., 1977.

INDEX